Islamic food with healing touch

بسم الله الرحمن الرحيم

Dedicated to
Late Janab Hakim Abdul Hamid Sahib

We are grateful to Welcom Hotel, Sheraton, New Delhi and Shalom, Greater Kailash, New Delhi for facilitating the photography.

ISBN: 978-81-7436-750-1

Published in India by Roli Books
in arrangement with Roli & Janssen BV
M-75, G.K. II Market;
New Delhi-110 048, India.
Phone: ++91-11-29212271, 40682000
Fax: ++91-11-29217185
Email: info@rolibooks.com
Website: rolibooks.com

Editor: Neeta Datta
Design: Devan Das
Pre press: Jyoti Dey
Production: Naresh Nigam & Shaji Sahdevan

Printed and bound in India by Replika Press Pvt. Ltd.

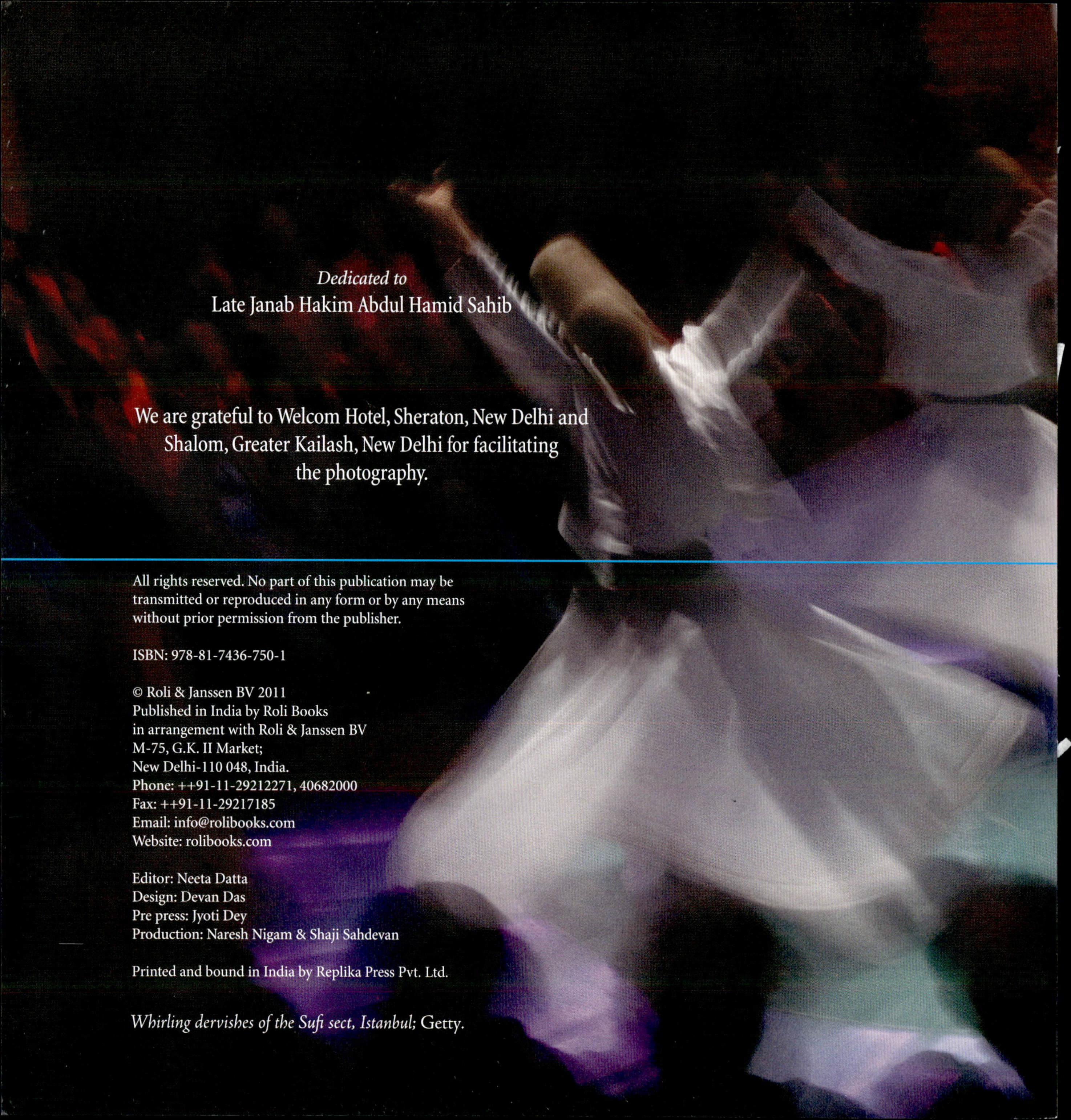

Whirling dervishes of the Sufi sect, Istanbul; Getty.

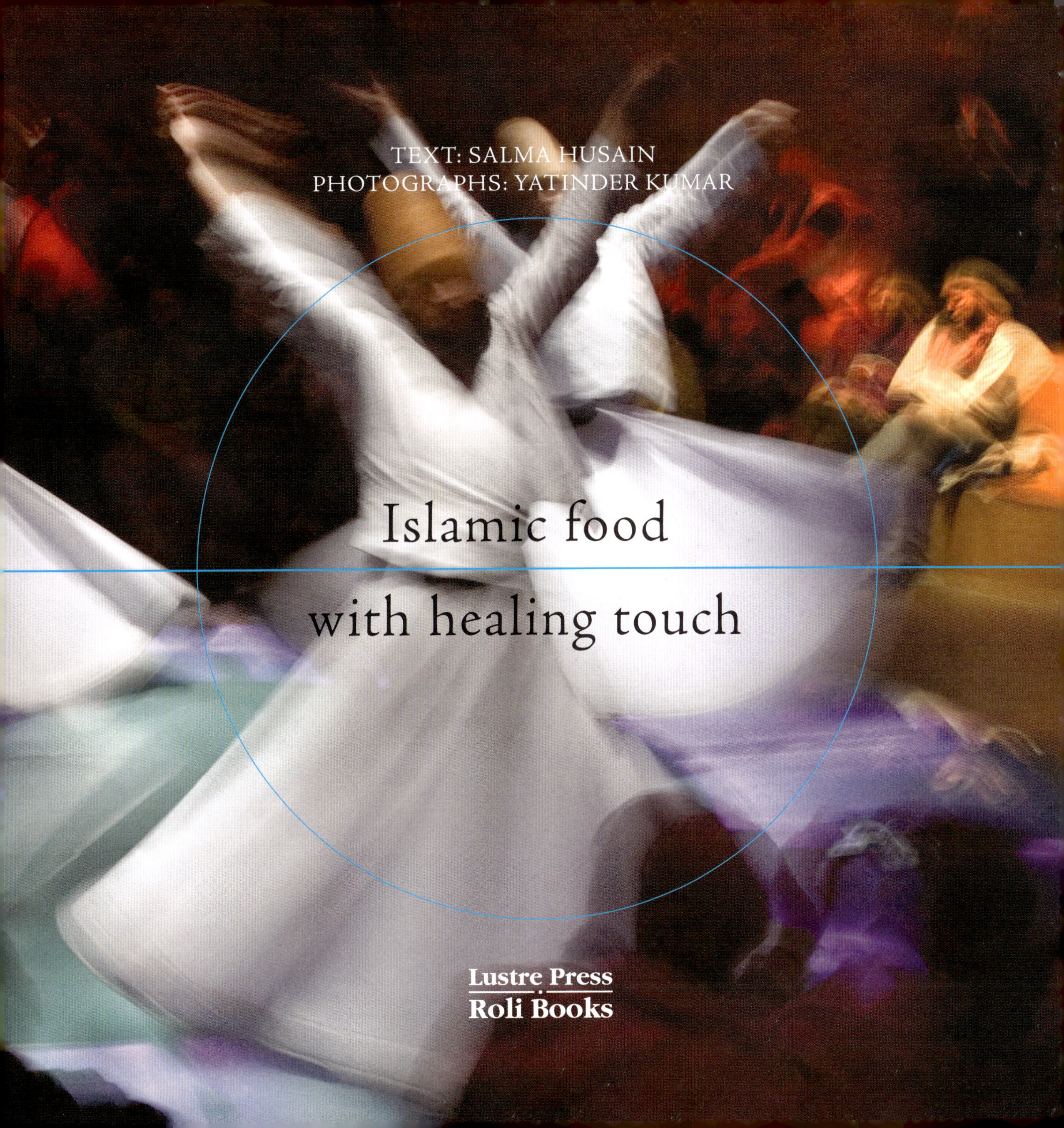

TEXT: SALMA HUSAIN
PHOTOGRAPHS: YATINDER KUMAR

Islamic food with healing touch

Lustre Press
Roli Books

Contents

Shah Abbas being served by a courtier (fresco); Getty.

Food in Islam

EARLY HISTORY OF ISLAMIC CUISINE

Before we talk about food in Islam, it is necessary to know a little about Islam and its dietary rules. A monotheistic religious system founded in the seventh century, and based on the teachings of the Prophet Mohammad, as laid down in the holy book of the Quran, Islam is a complete way of life. As such, diet plays a very important role in the daily life of a believer. There are many verses in the Quran which draw attention to the nature of life and invite believers to carefully study their bodies, their souls and their mutual relationship. As the human body is the greatest gift of God, humans are advised to take care of it. For this reason alone, Islam has prohibited certain foods due to their ill affects and permitted all other pure, clean foods. Islamic dietary guidelines suggest a balanced diet for the growth, strength and repairing of the body.

The Arabic word *halal* literally means proper and lawful, referring to food that is permitted under the guidelines found in the Quran. Islamic dietary law has selected quadrupeds like cattle, sheep, goats, camels and horses for consumption, along with chickens, ducks, game birds, etc. Both fresh and salt water fish, with scales, are also acceptable. These are *halal*, but they must also be *zabihah*, that is, slaughtered according to Islamic rituals, in order to be suitable for consumption. Slaughtering an animal according to these guidelines limits the pain it must endure. Fresh or naturally frozen vegetables, fresh or dried fruits, legumes like peanuts, cashew nuts, hazel nuts, walnuts, etc., are all *halal*, along with grains, such as wheat, rice, rye, barley, oats, etc. Milk, honey and any non-intoxicating plants are also allowed.

Haram refers to food that is unlawful under Islam. Some examples of *haram* include carnivorous animals, pigs (and their by-products), birds of prey and those which do not

Quran and the tasbih *(rosary).*

have talons but flap their wings more often, reptiles and insects. In addition, the blood of *halal* animals and its by-products is also *haram*. Like halal, *haram* extends to the method by which the animal has died, so those that have died, instead of being ritually slaughtered, are *haram*. Otherwise halal animals killed in the name of anyone other than Allah, or without the Islamic rites are also considered *haram*. Alcohol and other intoxicants are definitely *haram*.

Prior to the advent of Islam, the food of the Arabs was basic. Their daily diet included dates and either camel, sheep or goat milk, churned into butter and clarified for storing. Meat was a luxury: only gazelle, ibex or hare were hunted. With the advent of Islam, food habits changed and the dietary laws laid down in the Quran were followed. Certain foods of the time are mentioned by name in the Quran, and are known to have particularly beneficial powers. Squash is among the vegetables mentioned by the Prophet. Dried fruits are beneficial according to the Quran and Hadith. The Prophet also mentioned figs and then stated: "If I had to mention a fruit that descended from paradise I would say this is it because the paradisiacal fruits do not have pits ... eat from these fruits for they prevent hemorrhoid and help gout."

The spread of Islam following the death of the Prophet Muhammad in 632 changed the face of the tiny Islamic world. With revolutionary fervour, the Arabs from the Arabian peninsula swept into greater Syria and Persia conquering one territory after another, converting them into Islamic domains, until they had established a vast Islamic empire, spreading right across Asia and North Africa and into Sicily and Spain. Wherever they went they took their culinary traditions with them and adopted those of the conquered territories along the way, so a myriad dishes and flavours permeated the empire.

The new Islamic empire governed by the Umayyad dynasty of caliphs from Damascus is not much known for its culinary art. The majority of the Arabs remained nomads. They knew nothing of husbandry and agriculture, so milk and milk products formed their main diet. Milk was drunk warm straight after milking or thickened in a goat's skin—yoghurt was not introduced until after the conquest of Persia. Sometimes unleavened bread was made by grinding the grain in a stone quern, kneading it with a little water and shaping it into rounds. It was then baked on a metal dish heated on dried camel dung or dead tree branches. Very little meat was eaten, and dates were a favourite food.

However, some Arabian dishes, like *harīsa* became as famous and internationally known as pizza is today. This famous dish also travelled to England, where the name was translated into the English of the fourteenth century as *frumenty*, derived from the Middle French word for "grain". It became in England a kind of wheat stew boiled with milk, cinnamon, and sugar.

CUISINE OF THE CALIPHS

It was during the Abbasid period, from the eighth to the twelfth century, that Islam was the most powerful influence in the world. The expansion of Islam caused the spread of food that was formerly known to only one region. Rice, for example, originated in India and was introduced to Iran and Syria. Not all foods, however, could be grown readily in every region of the Muslim world, and this necessitated trade. These products were transported by ship or by caravan.

In general, middle and upper class family households had their own domestic kitchen, while less fortunate families had to make do with communal kitchens. Houses of this period had kitchens that were essentially open courtyards, with additional rooms used for storage, cook's quarters, and the like. The Abbasid kitchen was equipped with two main appliance —the *tannur* or oven and the *mustawkad* or stove. The *tannur*, which was used for baking resembled a large overturned pot. Charcoal was added via a hole in its side and lit, after which, the food to be baked was introduced. The temperature was regulated by opening or closing a vent at the top of the oven. A number of utensils evolved for use with a *tannur*—the rolling pin, a special poker to pick up food and a metal scraper for cleaning the oven after baking was finished, to name a few. *Tannur* was used to prepare casseroles and pies in addition to breads. The *mustawkad*, on the other hand, consisted of a fireplace built to accommodate multiple cooking pots at a height convenient for cooking. Utensils commonly found in the kitchen included clay pots, copper or stone, pans made from iron, skewers, knives especially for cutting meat and vegetables, and mortars.

A caliph's banquet with music and dance.

As with any culture, the storage of food was an important issue in Baghdad. Travellers, traders and armies could not always afford to take livestock with them, to be slaughtered when needed, having to rely instead on preserved provisions. Seasonal foods were often in demand throughout the year. The excess food could not be allowed to be wasted, and this gave rise to granaries. The grains were stored in silos or granaries and were protected from various pests. Fruits and vegetables were stored in airtight containers which were sometimes buried underground. Melons from Khwarzam were packed in ice and kept in lead containers while being transported. Meat was preserved by treating with salt and vinegar, but freshly slaughtered meat was preferred.

Baghdad saw great marriages of cooking styles and culinary art reached its zenith during the reign of Harun-al-Rashid (786-809) and his son Al-Mamun (813-833), a period in history which is vividly described in the pages of the *Arabian Nights* and similar literary works. With Mecca as the religious centre and Baghdad as its capital, the golden age of Islam began. It was a time of intellectual and cultural awakening and a rich period for culinary activities. Culinary literature attained the status of an art in the areas of both pleasure and health. The *Kitab-al-Tabikh al Warraq*, the earliest surviving book of the time, gives detailed accounts of the recipes, their ingredients and health properties, utensils and table manners. Besides recipes the book contains anecdotes about cooking contests organized by the Caliph.

The taste for special food and sweet things appeared during this period. Before that, spices had been only aromatic and were used in tiny quantities but in great number and varieties of combination. Baghdadi cuisine was rich with many herbs, five or six in one dish, and complex stews, often cooked in the *tannur* (tandoor oven). Some had Persian names, such as *sikbaaj* (which was flavoured with vinegar) and *naarbaaj* (flavoured with pomegranate juice). The dishes with Arabic names, presumably developed in Baghdad, were often named after the main ingredient; for example, *adasiyyah* (lentils with meat) and *shaljamiyyah* (with turnips). Some were named for aristocrats.

The royal banquets of the caliphs of Baghdad are legendary for their extravagancies. They amalgamated the peasant dishes of the area and the Bedouin foods of Syria. Lavish

dishes were invented, poems praising food were recited and diners ate to the sound of music and singing.

The cuisine of the caliphs was transformed; new culinary techniques were acquired from the conquered people and via trade routes beyond the empire. There came olive oil from Syria, dates from Iraq, coffee from Arabia, chefs came from Egypt, spices from India, Africa and China, but the strongest influence was of Persia.

PERSIAN CULINARY INFLUENCE

Persians have looked at food through three different lenses for many centuries: as medicinal, philosophical, and cultural. Physicians and philosophers considered food and beverages the main factors in reviving the human body. Consuming food was seen as a way of weakening or strengthening human character. The common philosophy of food having a hot or cold essence was linked to the ancient Zoroastrian religion of the area. This philosophy was once shared by other civilizations including China, India, and the medieval West. Culturally food was considered to be an art, providing enjoyment to both body and mind. All of these were strengthened by the advent of Islam.

Feasting in the meadows.

The seventh century Arab conquest of Persia, which introduced Islam to the population, was followed by invasions from Seljuk Turks and the Mongols. In Persia, Arabs found a sophisticated court with a rich and impressive cuisine, and they eagerly adopted Persian eating habits. Though no

Food being carried for a banquet in Persepolis.

accurate record of classical Persian cooking is available, it is clear that the ancient Persians cherished food. For instance, Emperor Darius paid special attention to agriculture and elaborate banquets were held in Persepolis. Walnuts, pistachios, pomegranates, cucumbers, broad beans and peas (known in China as the "Iranian bean"), basil, coriander, and sesame were introduced by Parthian and Sasanian traders. The techniques of cooking them have been passed down from generation to generation.

Contemporary Persian cooking wears its heritage on its sleeve. Arabs gave Iran the art of making bread, which is still baked in traditional tandoors. However, rice has the place of honour, sometimes containing almonds, pistachios, glazed carrots or orange peels, and raisins; other times finished with vegetables and spices; occasionally with meat. It is often perfected and finished by the use of specially-prepared saffron from Iran and cooked slowly after boiling to have a hard crust at the bottom (*tah dig*). Rice dishes are considered special by Persians, partly because rice has been rare, grown only in the northern Caspian provinces. Persia's delicious aromatic rice has won many admirers. Jewelled rice (*morasa polow*) was described as "the King of Persian dishes" by James Morier, the shrewd English diplomat who knew Qajar Persia well, and wrote *Haji Baba of Isfahan*, the best comic novel on Iran.

Every meal is accompanied by refreshing drinks called sharbats made from diluted fruit and herb syrups. It is not known when exactly the sharbat came into being, but the earliest records date from 200 B.C. to the Shiraz school of cooking in Persia. The first sharbat is said to have been of almonds topped with lukewarm water. This mixture was strained and chilled before serving in porous earthen containers, which kept it cool. Today, all over the Middle East and Indian sub-continent, sharbats play a very important role. They are cooling, energy giving, healing and pleasant to drink. Fruits, flowers, roots and vegetables can be used to make them.

A *samavar* (traditional tea jar) is an essential part of every household as tea ranks with *abdugh* (buttermilk) as Persia's principal beverage. It is served in small slender glasses with lumps of sugar.

Lamb and chicken are marinated and grilled as kababs, or mixed into stews called *khoreshes* with fruit and sour ingredients such as lime juice. Cinnamon, cardamom, and other spices are used in great abundance, along with a multitude of fresh herbs. They blend opposing flavours, such as sour grape juice with the sweetness of fresh fruits and spices. It is these flavours and the passion for fresh herbs, which make Persian cooking exquisite.

Ice creams have been known for centuries to the Persians, through a remarkable system that stored mountain ice underground through the hot months to provide cool drinks. Ice was not even a luxury.

THE OTTOMAN INFLUENCES

In 1258, the Abbasid caliphate fell at the hands of Mongols who enjoyed a short period of glory and were driven away. In the first half of the eleventh century a new scourge appeared: wild Turkish-speaking nomads entered Persia and under the Seljuks. They swept across Persia to Armenia, massacring, looting and raping as they went. The Seljuks occupied Baghdad, Syria and Egypt and then moved on to Asia Minor where they created the first Turkish Empire.

The enormous Ottoman Empire expanded into the heart of Europe from the fourteenth century and produced a new court cuisine in its turn. Under Suleyman the Magnificent (1520-68), the Ottoman Empire became a major naval power, and Constantinople the most beautiful city in the world.

Turkish cuisine has its roots in nomadic life, dependant on agriculture and breeding of animals. Central Asian migrants consumed meat prepared in *tandirs* (underground ovens) or grilled their meat on open fire. *Kovurma* are the small cubes of meat cooked in their own fat, salted and stored in earthenware containers

A vendor in Istanbul.

A portrait of Fatih Sultan Mehmat.

and eaten in winter. Meat was also salted and spiced, dried in the sun and consumed whenever required. The first Turkish-Arabic dictionary of cooking methods was prepared in the eleventh century and included the culinary styles of the nomadic Turks. These styles of cooking were easily subsumed into Islamic cuisine and continue to be in use today.

With the rise of the Ottoman Empire, Turkish cuisine reached its zenith and the Sultan's courts became notorious for their luxury and the pleasures of the table.

Trade relations brought new ingredients and, with the expansion of the empire, Ottoman cuisine was influenced by the urban life of Constantinople and the large number of slaves captured in battle. On the occasion of Suleyman's marriage, free breakfast was served to all: bread and olives for the poor; cheese, bread, fruit and rose petal jam for the middle class. Fruits from different parts of the empire, sharbats of lemon juice and snow, flavoured with honey, musk and amber, were served alongside water lilies together with sharbats made of violet, honey and squares of rice jelly sprinkled with rose water. All this was a mere seventy years after the empire was established.

The most rapid progress in Turkish cuisine was observed during the reign of Fatih Sultan Mehmat (1444-46 and 1451-81). Olive oil replaced butter. Sugar replaced honey or grape molasses; almost all kinds of spices and herbs such as fennel, mint, coriander, sesame, rose petals and saffron were being used in Turkish dishes for better taste, flavour and aroma.

The importance of culinary art to the Ottomans is evident to every visitor to the Topkapi Palace. The huge kitchen, distributed among several buildings, had ten domes by the seventeenth century. The kitchen staff–1,300 of them–were housed in the palace. Hundreds of cooks specialized in different types of food such as soup, pilaf, kababs, etc., and fed as many as 10,000 people a day. In the early days of the Ottoman Empire, all the palace cooks were slaves who had been captured or bought. To take advantage of their skills and safeguard their cooking art for the future, a cooking school was established for their children to educate them not only in cooking but also introduce them to the courtly etiquette of dining. The position of the cook was elevated and became a high rank in the courts. It is interesting to note that Koprulu Mehmet Pasha, the Ottoman Empire's most powerful sultan, started his career as a cook.

Following the example of the palace, all the grand Ottoman houses boasted elaborate kitchens and competed in preparing feasts for each other as well as for the general public. This is how the traditional cuisine evolved and spread even to the most modest corners of the country.

The first Turkish-born cooks employed in Topkapi Palace were recruited as camp cooks from Bolu, in northwestern Anatolia, where the sultans went hunting. It became a tradition that every boy of the age of thirteen would work in the palace kitchen or in the houses of the nobles in Constantinople.

It is said that finest kabab dishes are found in Anatolia, Armenia, and the Caucasus where people in the villages still cook their meals in the charcoal burning clay oven, which are sunk into the ground and called *tandir.* This is, perhaps, the most original, and in some respects, the oldest method of cooking. It was on the mountain ranges of the Caucasus that the art of cutting meat into small portions and marinating it in oil flavoured with spices and herbs was first developed.

After 400 years of glory, Ottoman Empire fell leaving behind the glorious culinary legacy. Turkish cuisine is still regarded as one of the greatest in the world as its culinary traditions have survived for over 1,300 years, influencing Islamic cuisine worldwide.

SUFI CUISINE

The Seljuk Turks settled down in Konya, from where they ruled Greater Syria. Konya became the centre of attraction for poets, scholars and mystics, and also developed a

A whirling dervish

Sufi cuisine. To Mevlana Rumi the great mystic, food was the spontaneous language of ecstasy. The Mevlevi dervish order he founded in Konya is shot through with food. In the era before, the dervish *tariqats* (Sufi path) were closed; the kitchen was the heart of a Mevlevi lodge. The chief spiritual adviser was the Asçõ Dede, or Cook Father, who also oversaw the mundane workings of the kitchen.

Mevlana Rumi wrote in Persian, and referred to many specific foods, some of which have survived to the present day, in name if not in every detail of their preparation. Some of his references include chickpeas; eggplant (Mevlana wasn't fond of it); spinach; onions, garlic and vinegar; wheat and barley; butter and buttermilk; pickles, peaches and pomegranates. Specific dishes he wrote about read like a menu of contemporary Islamic cuisine. They include *lablabu*, or roasted chickpeas; the noodle dish *tutmaj*, *yakhni*, a generic term for lamb stew; kababs; *harisa-ye-rasida*, a porridge made of grains and meat; boiled ox-feet; *sanbusa*, meat turnovers; biryani, a dish of rice, meat and vegetables; *qadid*, or dried spiced meat; *tharid*, boiled meat or bread and gravy; rice pudding; *luzina*, or nut candies, *jowzina*, or sugared almonds; *paluda*, a dish of milk, flour and spices; *kadayif*, a pastry made of shredded wheat, nuts and syrup; and the much-beloved *halvah*, a generic word for a range of sweets for the most part based on fried flour (reference Rumi's kitchen).

Legends credit him with the opening posture of the Mevlevi devotional dance. Ateþ-Baz, the cook, had complained that he hadn't enough wood for cooking, so Mevlana told him to put his feet under the stove in place of the wood, and his toes obligingly emitted fire. But because he had doubted, his left big toe was burned, and he covered it in shame. This is said to be the reason that the Mevlevis begin their *sema* with the toes of the right foot over those of the left. The tomb of his cook has become a shrine for gastronomic pilgrimage (reference *Sufi Cuisine* by Nevin Helici).

One of the traditional roles of the dervish lodge was as community kitchen and hostel, providing food and shelter for the poor and travellers. Many early Sufis were "sons of the road", wandering during the warm season, and relying on the grace of God and the spontaneous generosity of fellow Sufis for shelter and sustenance. Followers of other faiths also could count on such generosity, with no questions asked about their religion.

A kitchen in which meals were cooking around the clock was the hallmark of many Sufi saints. The great Chishti Shaikh Nizamuddin Auliya was known to entertain large groups of travelling dervishes—even thirty or more—for up to three days at a time. The three-day limit is in keeping with Muhammad's counsel: "Hospitality extends for three days, and anything beyond that is charity."

The desire to share food was one basis for the development of communities—the Turkish word *tekke* referred to a refectory or dining hall long before it became exclusively identified with a Sufi establishment. With the development of orders and communities came a greater capacity to serve greater numbers; but no matter what its size, each Sufi centre had lodgings reserved for guests, and a place of honour for them at the table.

Following the example of their founder, Muinuddin Chishti, Chishti Khanqahs have always kept open kitchens and have provided vital services in public emergencies. For centuries the Ajmer Langar Khana has cooked and distributed twice daily a barley porridge, itself known as *langar*.

Mevlevi cuisine also includes Central Asian contributions such as *börek*, *tutmaç* noodles and the humble flour soup *bulamaç aþõ*. One exceptionally interesting and delicious dish is *belh-ozbek pilav*, which entered the tradition because it comes from Balkh, Mevlana's ancestral home in northern Afghanistan. It is made with meat, chickpeas and carrots and resembles what the Turks today call *buhara pilavõ*, except that this version is enriched with pine nuts and chestnuts. It also contains currants, which probably stand in for the barberries used in Central Asia.

THE KITCHEN OF CORDOBA

By 718 the Muslims had taken control of most of Spain. In the tenth century, the great Andalusian city of Cordoba had a population of half a million. It had lighted streets, libraries with hundreds of thousands of volumes, some 700 mosques and 900 public baths. The homes of the wealthy had fountains, plumbing and running water. Cities of the Near

East, North Africa, and Moorish Spain were supported by elaborate agricultural systems which included extensive irrigation based on the knowledge of hydraulic and hydrostatic principles, some of which were continued from Roman times. Spain in turn transmitted these to the rest of Europe along with many agricultural and fruit-growing processes, new plants, fruit and vegetables. These new crops included sugarcane, rice, citrus fruit, apricots, cotton, artichokes, aubergines, and saffron.

Drink vendors were everywhere, proffering tea perfumed with fresh mint, a dash of rose water or orange blossom. Meat balls called *miraga*, fried fish and a kind of cheese cake called *almojabana* were noisily hawked at food stalls. The marketplaces were full of vegetables, fruits, lamb and veal meat, a variety of game and fish, particularly tuna, shad and sardine, and literally thousands of aromatic herbs and spices.

In the court kitchens of Cordoba and Granada, cooks could now produce the dishes of high Islamic cuisine. There were the *pilaus*, made by frying rice or thin wheat noodles and then simmering them in an aromatic liquid until it was fully absorbed. Another family of dishes consisted of delicate dumplings (*albondigas*) made of meat pounded with seasonings. And there were the most characteristic meat dishes: meltingly tender spicy stews. Flavoured with a variety of herbs and spices, these stews were cooked in earthenware pots nestled in circular holes in charcoal-heated masonry bench stoves. Some were green with spinach and coriander. Others were golden with saffron. And the most complex were flavoured with cinnamon, cloves, peppercorns, almonds and raisins and thickened with eggs or bread crumbs. Other great creations of the Muslim kitchen were based on clarified white sugar. Sweetened drinks (sharbats) were flavoured with ground nuts, citrus fruits and pomegranates. Jams were made of rose petals, oranges and apricots, and dense pastes of quinces. Figurines were modelled from a white paste of sugar mixed with gum (*alfenique*). And a wide variety of confections such as marzipan was created from sugar and nuts.

MUGHAL CULINARY INFLUENCE

In 1526 Babur established the Mughal dynasty in India and his successors ruled Hindustan for 300 years. They left behind a legacy of food, which has not lost its colour till date. This era saw a flowering of native poetry and art, and its rarified cooking, with rich sauces and pilafs strewn with nuts and dried fruit became the foundation of the Mughal cuisine of northern India. They brought with them the exotic heritage of Persian and Turkish cuisine and influenced both the style and substance of Indian food, enriching native cuisine with nuts, raisins cream and butter. They added to the melting pot of Indian cuisine with new exotic dishes like *paththar kabab, haleem, aash*, various kinds of pulaos and kababs. They also had a refined and courtly etiquette of sharing food in fellowship.

These emperors were patron of gastronomy and their patronage took culinary art to its utmost zenith. With the fall of the Mughal Empire, the cooks tried to find refuge with other courts and spread their expertise across the sub-continent, accounting to some extent, for the similarity of food across Pakistan, Bangladesh and India even today.

Preparations for a Mughal banquet; National Museum of India.

THE ISLAMIC FEAST

Like any other religion, the time of the year plays a very important role in the life of a Muslim. The Islamic calendar or Hijri calendar is a lunar calendar based on twelve lunar months in a year of 354 or 355 days, used to date events in many Muslim countries, and used by Muslims everywhere to determine the proper day on which various festivals fall.

Ramadan refers to the ninth month in the Muslim calendar. Every Muslim is expected to fast during the day for the entire lunar month. During the blessed month of Ramadan, Muslims all over the world abstain from food, drink, and other physical needs during the

Breaking of fast (iftar); *Corbis.*

daylight hours. As a time to purify the soul, refocus attention on God, and practice self-sacrifice, Ramadan is much more than just not eating and drinking.

Fasting during Ramadan is strictly adhered to in countries where there's a large Islamic population. During this month, keeping in mind the season, special dishes are prepared for breaking of the fast (*iftar*), which is often an elaborate affair. Similarly, Eid-ul-Fitr, the day marking the end of the fasting month is spent eating and drinking special dishes, which are made only on this big day. The focus at Eid celebrations is a huge family meal of favourite dishes like biryani, pulao, qorma, sheer khurma in India and, in the Arab world, *gouzy* which is spectacular and much-feted dish of stuffed roasted lamb with a highly seasoned pulao in which roast chickens nestle.

It is difficult to encompass the entire culinary sphere of Islamic civilization, which covers a vast landscape with endlessly varied tastes and abundance and scarcity being locked in perpetual rivalry.

Many countries have contributed to the enrichment of Islamic cuisine, keeping in mind the dietary laws of Islam. Each country has its own flavour, its own ingredients and its own culture. The cooking is different in every town and village, indeed in every family. There are rural foods and foods which belong to the desert, the mountains, the plains or the sea coast. Though the cooking differs with each place, there are many general characteristics which these foods and all the countries share.

Islamic cuisine employs a very sensual kind of cooking, using herbs, spices, and aromatics generously. Certain methods like slow cooking over charcoal or long, slow simmering in sun glazed covered pots, or baking in a tandoor are typical of Islamic cooking. Many Muslim countries have common elements in their cuisine, serving stuffed vegetables, meat balls, scented rice puddings, pies wrapped in paper-thin pastries or leaves, and fritters soaked in syrup.

In short, the rich heritage of Islam has given the world a unique legacy in the form of its cuisine.

Shorba, Salaat aur Kabab

(Soups, Salads & Kababs)

Shorba is a common dish in Muslim cuisine, it is widely cooked in most parts of the Middle Eastern countries such as Syria, Turkey, Iraq, and Iran as one-meal-dish, and is called by different names such as *chorba*, *shorva*, and *shorba*. They make an excellent dish for breaking of the Ramadan fast. In India and Pakistan, rich aromatic *shorba*, *nahari*, and *paye ka shorba* make excellent winter breakfast. *Shorba* has varied texture, ranging from simple vegetable to meat. Poultry, lentils, chickpeas, beans, and peas as well as fruits and nuts are added to it. Yoghurt and lentil *shorbas* are also popular and are enjoyed by all.

Salaat feature prominently in Muslim cuisine. They are delightfully refreshing and appetite stimulating. In serving a salad, colour, texture and presentation is most important. The four basic dressing ingredients are–olive oil, lemon juice, vinegar, and yoghurt as all of them have healing properties and satisfy the health enthusiast.

Though there are several kinds of savories and boreks, which are a popular feature of Muslim cuisine but **kababs** remain the most wanted and popular of them all. Kababs are an integral part of every celebration like birth of a child, wedding in the family, anniversary, a small gathering at home, or a big banquet. Ancient civilization knew all about grilling meats of all kinds on fire. Much later the art of marinating, basting, cooking on griddle and tandoor became common. Often they make one-meal-dish. This little piece of meat has travelled wide and reached India via Central Asia with the Mughals and got refined further.

Aash-e-Joe

A Bedouin favourite. This soup has many benefits. It is a thirst quencher and acts as a diuretic.

INGREDIENTS

SERVES 4

750 gm / 26 oz
Lamb (neck or shoulder with bone), cut into chunky pieces

1 cup / 200 gm / 7 oz
Chickpeas (*kabuli chana*), washed, soaked overnight

8 cups / 2 lt / 64 fl oz
Water

¾ cup Barley (*jowar*), washed, soaked overnight

¼ cup / 50 gm / 1¾ oz
Yellow lentil (*arhar dal*), washed

Salt to taste

Black peppercorns (*sabut kali mirch*), freshly ground, to taste

1 tbsp / 15 ml Olive oil

1 Onion, large, sliced

1 tsp / 3 gm Turmeric (*haldi*) powder

1 tsp Mint (*pudina*), dried

METHOD

- Boil the lamb in a large pot with 8 cups water. Add chickpeas along with the water in which it was soaked and bring slowly to simmer; skimming when necessary. Cover and simmer for 1 hour.
- Add barley, lentil, salt, and black pepper; mix well and bring the mixture to the boil.
- Remove the lamb from the pot, cool and strip from bones. Break the meat into small pieces and return them to the pot, cover and leave for 10 minutes.
- Heat the oil in another pot; add the onion and fry till golden brown. Sprinkle turmeric powder and fry until the onion is crisp. Remove and reserve.
- Rub mint into powder and sprinkle it into the pot, stir and remove from heat.
- Stir half the onion mixture into the soup, ladle the soup into bowls garnished with remaining onion mixture. Serve with bread.

Havuc Corbasi

A wonder soup from Anatolia with a creamy texture and a delicate flavour. This soup has a particularly beneficial effect on the liver.

INGREDIENTS

SERVES 4

450 gm / 1 lb Carrots (*gajar*), peeled, chopped into small pieces

¼ cup / 50 gm / 1¾ oz Butter

1.2 lt / 2 pints Water

Salt to taste

½ tsp / 1½ gm Black pepper (*kali mirch*) powder

1 tsp / 3 gm Sugar

½ tsp / 1½ gm Dilweed

1 tbsp / 10 gm Refined flour (*maida*)

5 tbsp / 75 ml / 3½ fl oz Milk

2 Egg yolks

2 tbsp / 20 gm Walnuts (*akhrot*), finely chopped for garnishing

METHOD

- Melt half the butter in a saucepan; add the carrots and sauté until well coated with butter. Add 300 ml / ½ pint water together with salt, black pepper powder, sugar, and dilweed. Bring to the boil and simmer until carrots are soft.
- Drain the carrots retaining little liquid to help purée them, if necessary. Make a smooth purée of carrots.
- Bring 1.2 lt / 2 pint water to the boil and add to the carrot purée; stirring continuously.
- Melt the remaining butter and remove from heat. Stir in flour and add milk slowly stirring until smooth. Return to heat stirring continuously until the mixture is thick. Remove from heat and add egg yolks; blend well. Add the carrot purée, blend well.
- Serve hot garnished with chopped walnuts.

Harira

This thick soup of vegetable and pulses has been adopted by the Muslim Arab as their traditional breakfast meal during Ramadan. It was invented by the Berbers.

INGREDIENTS

SERVES 6

½ cup / 100 gm / 3½ oz Chickpeas (*kabuli chana*), soaked overnight

½ cup / 100 gm / 3½ oz Green gram (*moong dal*)

1 tbsp / 15 gm Butter

225 gm / 8 oz Lamb, cut into cubes

1 Onion, chopped

450 gm / 1 lb Tomatoes, peeled, chopped

1 Celery leaf, chopped

2 tbsp / 8 gm Parsley, fresh, chopped

1 tbsp / 4 gm Green coriander (*hara dhaniya*), chopped

½ tsp / 3 gm Ginger (*adrak*), grounded

½ tsp / 1½ gm Turmeric (*haldi*) powder

1 tsp / 3 gm Cinnamon (*dalchini*), grounded

Salt and freshly ground black pepper (*kali mirch*) to taste

2 Egg yolks

1 Juice of lemon (*nimbu*)

Green coriander, chopped for garnishing

METHOD

- Drain the chickpeas, rinse under cold water and set aside.
- Melt the butter in a large saucepan and fry the lamb and onion for 2-3 minutes, stirring, until the lamb is just browned. Add the tomatoes, all the herbs and spices and season well with salt and black pepper, cook for about a minute and then pour in 1¾ lt water. Add the lentils and chickpeas.
- Slowly bring to the boil and remove the surplus froth. Boil rapidly for 10 minutes, then reduce the heat and simmer very gently until the chickpeas are very tender. Season with salt and a little more pepper if needed.
- Beat the egg yolks with lemon juice and stir into the simmering soup. Immediately remove the soup from the heat and stir until thickened. Pour into warmed serving bowls and serve garnished with green coriander, lemon slices and chopped walnuts.

Jajik

A refreshing salad and a wonder food which helps to restore strength. It is mentioned in the *Book of Wisdom* that Mevlana Rumi was fond of yoghurt with garlic.

INGREDIENTS

SERVES 4

2 Cucumbers (*khira*), peeled, diced

2 cups / 500 gm / 1.1 lb Yoghurt (*dahi*)

1 tbsp / 15 ml Olive oil

1 Garlic (*lasan*) clove, crushed

2 tbsp / 8 gm Mint (*pudina*), fresh, chopped

2 tbsp / 25 gm Green onion (*hara pyaz*), chopped

Salt to taste

METHOD

- Pour the yoghurt in a bowl and blend it with olive oil, garlic, mint, green onion, and salt.
- Add cucumber and mix well, until everything is well coated with yoghurt. Refrigerate for an hour and serve.

Cucumber

Cucumber is 95% water and so keeps the body hydrated and helps regulate the body's inner temperature. It also helps the body to flush out toxins. The skin contains vitamin C and can be used to relieve sunburn and mild skin irritations.

Fattoush

The respect for bread is general throughout the Muslim world, as for centuries people's existence was chiefly dependent on this. *Fattoush* is a colourful salad with an unusual texture and the essentials of *sumac's* uniquely lemony taste flavour the naturally sun-ripen tomatoes.

INGREDIENTS

SERVES 4

4 slices Bread, dried / toasted

6 Lettuce leaves, crisp, broken into small pieces

2 Tomatoes, seeded, chopped

1 Green pepper (*Shimla mirch*), cored, seeded, chopped

1 Red pepper, cored, seeded, chopped

1 tbsp / 4 gm Parsley, finely chopped

4 Spring onions (*hara pyaz*), finely chopped

1 tbsp / 4 gm Mint (*pudina*), fresh, finely chopped

1 Garlic (*lasan*) clove, crushed

1 Cucumber (*khira*), peeled, cut into chunks

For the dressing:

Salt and freshly ground black pepper (*kali mirch*) to taste

4 tbsp / 60 ml / 2 fl oz Olive oil extra virgin

2 tbsp / 30 ml / 1 fl oz Lemon (*nimbu*) juice

1 tbsp / 15 ml Boiling water

2 tbsp / 15 gm *Sumac* powder (see note)

METHOD

- Place the tomatoes in a bowl, sprinkle salt and pepper and leave aside for 10 minutes.
- In a large bowl, place the lettuce leaves. Add green pepper, red pepper, parsley, spring onions, mint, garlic, cucumber, and tomatoes. Add the bread slices and mix gently.
- **For the dressing**, mix all the ingredients mentioned together, except *sumac* powder. Shake well to combine and pour over the salad. Toss gently to combine.
- Garnish with mint and sprinkle with *sumac* powder. Let it stand for 5 minutes and serve chilled.

Note: Sumac *is a berry which is dried and crushed to form a coarse purple-red powder. It is used widely in Arabia, Turkey and Lebanese cuisine. It is a major souring agent.*

Chukander ka Raita

A popular yoghurt relish from India, Iran and other parts of Middle East. *Chukander ka raita* is a feast for the eyes, refreshing to eat, and a good tonic.

INGREDIENTS

SERVES 4

3 cups / 750 gm / 26 oz Yoghurt (*dahi*)

2 Beetroots (*chukander*), medium-sized, boiled, peeled, cut into small pieces

Black peppercorns (*sabut kali mirch*), freshly ground, to taste

Salt to taste

1 tbsp / 4 gm Mint (*pudina*), chopped

a dash Lemon (*nimbu*) juice

Dried mint (*pudina*) for garnishing

METHOD

- Whisk the yoghurt in a bowl; add beetroot (reserving ¼ cup), salt and pepper.
- Add a dash of lemon juice to sharpen the flavour. Blend in mint, cover and chill.
- Serve garnished with reserved beetroot and mint leaves.

Beetroot

Beetroot is beneficial for liver diseases and helps make red corpuscles in the body. It improves the skin and relieves pain of the stone in the kidney. The juice is a rich source of natural sugar and reduces blood pressure. The iron contained in beetroot is organic and non irritating, and will not cause constipation. This vegetable is so highly valued that it is said that it was offered on a silver platter to Apollo at Delphi.

Kasbi Mishwi

Organs of animal are delicacies for the Muslims and is enjoyed by young and old. As compared to other parts of the animal, liver, heart and neck has more nutrition.

INGREDIENTS

SERVES 4

900 gm / 2 lb Lamb liver, soaked in cold water for 20 minutes then drained

For the marinade:

5-6 Garlic (*lasan*) cloves, crushed

1½ tsp Mint (*pudina*), dried

½ cup / 120 ml / 4 fl oz Vegetable oil

1½ tsp / 4½ gm Salt

½ tsp / 1½ gm Black pepper (*kali mirch*)

Lemon wedges for garnishing

METHOD

- Remove any skin and sinew from the liver and then cut into 5 cm / 2" cubes.
- Mix all the ingredients of the marinade together in a large bowl. Add the pieces of liver and mix until well coated. Cover and set aside at room temperature for about 30 minutes.
- Thread on to skewers and cook over charcoal, turning frequently, for 8-10 minutes. Do not overcook or the liver will dry out and become hard.
- Serve with a little of the remaining marinade spooned over the top and garnished with lemon wedges.

Meat

The importance of meat protein in the human diet is clearly mentioned in the Quran: "And the cattle, He has created them for you, in them there is warmth (clothing) and numerous benefits, and of them you eat." Liver and cod liver oil are nutrient-packed super food supplement that can help boost energy, libido, muscle growth, brain powder and general health.

Sate Madura

This is the most common satay in Indonesia, originating in the island of Madura just to the northeast of Java. Easy-to-make and delicious to eat.

INGREDIENTS

SERVES 4-6

750 gm / 26 oz Lamb leg, cut into 2 cm cubes

¼ cup / 50 ml / 1¾ fl oz Sweet soy sauce

1 tbsp / 4 gm Green coriander (*hara dhaniya*), crushed

a pinch White peppercorns (*sabut safed mirch*), crushed

½ tsp / 2½ ml Lemon (*nimbu*) juice

2 Onions, peeled, sliced

METHOD

- Thread the lamb cubes onto satay skewers. Combine all the other ingredients except onions, mixing well. Dip each skewer in this sauce, using a spoon to help cover the meat well. Drain then grill the satay over hot charcoal.
- Combine the remaining sauce with onions and serve as a dip for the cooked satay.

Muslim influence

Arab traders ultimately converted Java from Hinduism to Islam and exercised their culinary influence as well. Kababs, marinated meat cubes threaded on skewers, were reinterpreted to become satay. Dill and fennel entered the repertoire of spices. Today Indonesia is the largest Muslim country in the world.

Djaaj Mishwi

A Lebanese delicacy served with garlic sauce which makes a delicious accompaniment to this dish.

INGREDIENTS

SERVES 4

2 Chickens, small, tender, cut into quarters

8 Garlic (*lasan*) cloves, crushed

Salt to taste

1 Juice of lemon (*nimbu*)

1 cup / 250 ml / 8 fl oz Olive oil

For the garlic sauce: makes 2½ cups

1 pod Garlic

1 tsp / 3 gm Salt

2 cups / 500 ml / 16 fl oz Olive oil

¼ cup / 60 ml / 2 fl oz Lemon juice

METHOD

- Mix the garlic, salt, lemon juice, and olive oil to make a marinade. Reserve ¼ cup and rub the remaining marinade over the chicken.
- Barbecue or grill the chicken, basting with the reserve marinade.
- **For the garlic sauce**, crush the garlic with salt in a mortar and pestle until the salt is dissolved. Gradually add olive oil, few drops at a time. Then add few drops of lemon juice; blend well till the oil and lemon juice are completely absorbed in the garlic The mixture should be light and fluffy like whipped cream. If it's not, then add some mashed potato.
- Serve the chicken hot with garlic sauce.

Glorious Garlic

One of the world's oldest healing food. It is a potent antiseptic. Evidence of its healing powers is detailed in the 4,000-year-old Sumerian records. Depiction of garlic bulbs have been discovered on the walls of the Egyptian tombs that dates back to 3,200 B C. Hippocrates, Father of Medicine, recommended garlic for infectious diseases and intestinal disorder.

Shami Kabab

A popular variety of kabab which flourished in the imperial kitchen of the Mughals. It travelled all over India and Pakistan to become the most favourite of all kababs. No celebration is complete without this kabab.

INGREDIENTS

SERVES 4

400 gm / 14 oz Lamb minced

⅓ cup / 65 gm / 2¼ oz Bengal gram (*chana dal*), picked, washed

4 Cloves (*laung*)

1 Brown cardamom (*badi elaichi*)

½" Cinnamon (*dalchini*) stick

1 Bay leaf (*tej patta*)

1 tsp / 6 gm Garlic (*lasan*) paste

½ tsp / 3 gm Ginger (*adrak*) paste

1 Potato, medium-sized

½ tsp / 1½ gm Red chilli powder

Salt to taste

½ tbsp / 7½ gm Yoghurt (*dahi*)

¼ tsp Vegetable oil

2 Green chillies, chopped

¼ cup / 15 gm Green coriander (*hara dhaniya*), finely chopped

1 Onion, finely chopped

¼ cup / 15 gm Mint (*pudina*), fresh, finely chopped

METHOD

- Cook the lamb with the next 10 ingredients. Add 2 cups water and bring the mixture to the boil, cover and simmer, on low heat, until the mince is tender and the mixture is dry. Stir twice while simmering. Keep aside to cool.
- Take out the potato from the mince. Remove skin and break into small pieces. Discard whole spices.
- Grind the mince mixture with potato on a stone grinder to a fine paste, without water or blend in a blender. Remove the mixture and place it on a tray, knead to soft dough, by adding yoghurt and oil.
- Mix green chillies, green coriander, onion, mint, and a pinch of salt together.
- Divide the lamb mixture into 8 equal portions. Flatten each portion, and make a patty, fill with the green chilli mixture.
- Shallow-fry the patties on a griddle. Serve with onion rings and lemon wedges

Gosht aur Sabzi

(Non Vegetarian & Vegetarian)

Lamb, poultry and **fish** are used popularly to make the main dishes of Muslim cuisine perfectly balanced with herbs and few spices to preserve the natural flavour of the main ingredients and make it easy-to-digest. These dishes are not covered with mask of sauces and tons of oils but are often combined with vegetables and aromatic herbs to enhance the flavour.

Lamb remains the favoured meat of the Muslims, and features prominently in the *Arabian Nights* as a delightful and sumptuous food. Its mention highlights its status as food for the elite. *The Tale of the Porter* and the *Three Ladies of Baghdad*, includes a comic lamentation poem about a magnificent feast. This feast has several lamb dishes. The first is a lamb pudding with wheat paste and spices, also the most commonly mentioned dish in the *Arabian Nights*.

"A table without **vegetables** is like an old man devoid of wisdom." This is a famous Arab saying. It is also mentioned in the Quran: "It is He who sends down rain from the sky, and with it we bring forth vegetation of all kinds, and out of it we bring forth thick clustered grains…".Eating fresh vegetables of the season with fresh bread is a satisfying meal in itself. Vegetables help to accelerate digestion. Whenever possible use fresh vegetables and only when not available resort to frozen or tinned version.

Harisah

This recipe has been taken from an old Arabic cookbook of *Ibn al-Mabrad.* It is a traditional dish and cooked on festive occasions. In Turkey it is called *keskek* and in Lebanon and Syria it is *harisah.* In India it is called *haris*, but the origin is from Anatolia. Adopted by all with regional variations.

INGREDIENTS

SERVES 4

500 gm / 1.1 lb Lamb, cleaned, washed, cut into pieces

2 cups / 500 ml / 16 fl oz Water

½" Cinnamon (*dalchini*) stick

Salt to taste

1 cup / 200 gm / 7 oz Cracked wheat (*dalia*), washed, soaked in water for 2 hours, drained

½ cup / 125 ml / 4 fl oz Milk

¼ tsp Cumin (*jeera*) powder

½ tsp / 1½ gm Cinnamon powder

½ tsp / 2½ ml Lemon (*nimbu*) juice

METHOD

- Cook the lamb adding water, cinnamon stick, and salt. Bring to the boil, reduce heat and cook until the lamb is half done. Add the cracked wheat and cook for another hour until meat is soft and tender and wheat is soft and mushy.
- Remove the lamb, strip the meat from the bones, pound in a mortar almost to a paste, then put it back and mix well with the wheat mixture. The mixture should have a thick porridge-like consistency.
- Add milk and simmer for 10 minutes. Season with salt, cumin powder, cinnamon powder, and lemon juice. Serve with a dollop of butter.

NOTE: *If using pressure cooker the cooking time would be reduced to 30 minutes for meat and 20 minutes for wheat. A traditional* harisah *dish is cooked overnight and eaten in the morning.*

Buran

This dish is named after the bride of caliph Al-Ma'mun. The wedding was in 825 A D (222 AH, the Islamic era). Today a vast range of dishes called *burani* or *buraniyyah* are made everywhere from Spain to India.

INGREDIENTS

SERVES 4-6

1 Eggplant (*baingan*)

3 tbsp / 45 ml / 1½ fl oz Sesame (*til*) oil

6 tbsp / 90 gm / 3 oz Yoghurt (*dahi*)

2 Garlic (*lasan*) cloves, crushed

Salt to taste

1 tsp / 3 gm Coriander (*dhaniya*) powder

500 gm / 1.1 lb Lamb mince

¼ cup / 40 gm / 1¼ oz Sheep fat (optional)

Refined oil for frying

½ tsp / 1½ gm Cumin (*jeera*) and cinnamon (*dalchini*) powder

METHOD

- Boil the eggplant for 5 minutes in water with salt. Let it drain, cool and dry.
- Heat the oil in a casserole; stew the eggplant on low heat, covered, until it is very soft (30-45 minutes). Turn the eggplant a couple of times.
- Pull the skin off the eggplant, and mince the flesh with a fork or in a blender. Temper with yoghurt, garlic, salt, and coriander powder.
- Form small balls of the minced lamb and sheep fat (optional) adding salt and pepper and place them on a flat dish snugly.
- Heat the oil and fry the meat balls till brown in colour. Remove and drain.
- Pour enough water to cover the balls and simmer until the water has evaporated. Add the eggplant sauce to the meat balls and heat through.
- Sprinkle cumin and cinnamon powder just before serving. If you want to add some colour, garnish with fresh green coriander.

Tharid

A traditional Bedouin braised meat popular in pre-Islamic and early Islamic period. A complete meal, full of energy, for the hard Bedouin life. This special dish is usually made on religious holidays such as the Prophet's birthday.

INGREDIENTS

SERVES 4-6

1 kg / 2.2 lb
Lamb / Beef, boneless, stewed, cut into cubes

2 Onions, large, chopped

2 tbsp / 30 gm / 1 oz
Ghee / Oil

2 tsp / 6 gm
Baharat (see note)

1 Garlic (*lasan*) clove

2 cups Tomatoes, chopped

½ cup / 100 gm / 3½ oz
Tomato paste

Salt to taste

½ tsp / 1½ gm
Black pepper (*kali mirch*), freshly ground

¼ cup / 15 gm
Parsley, chopped

750 gm / 26 oz Potatoes, peeled, halved if large

1 flat Bread

Parsley chopped for garnishing

METHOD

- Heat the ghee / oil in a heavy-based pan; add the onions and gently fry until transparent. Increase heat and add the meat cubes. Stir until meat loses its red colour. Add spices and garlic and cook for a minute.
- Add tomatoes, tomato paste, salt, black pepper, and parsley. Cover and simmer very gently for 1½ hours.
- Add the potatoes to the pan, cover and simmer for further 1½ hours.
- Cut the bread into small pieces and place in a serving dish. Ladle meat, potatoes and sauce on top and sprinkle with chopped parsley.
- Serve with salad and pickles.

Note: Baharat *is a mixture of spices used in the Gulf, Arabic and Iraqi cooking. It is a combination of cinnamon, clove, nutmeg, cumin, coriander, and pepper with paprika added for colour.*

Gulai Daging Lembu

Tenderly simmered meat offers the typical Malaysian taste of coconut balanced with tangy spices and delicate flavour of star anise.

INGREDIENTS

SERVES 4

600 gm / 22 oz Beef / Lamb, cleaned thoroughly, cut into bite-sized pieces

1 cup / 250 ml / 8 fl oz Water

5 tbsp / 35 gm / 1 oz Meat curry powder

½ cup / 125 ml / 4 fl oz Refined oil

6 Shallots, ground

4 Garlic (*lasan*) cloves, ground to paste

3 cm piece Ginger (*adrak*), ground to paste

2 Cloves (*laung*)

2 tbsp / 25 gm Coconut (*nariyal*), grated, fried until golden and pounded

1 Star anise (*chakri ke phool*)

1½" Cinnamon (*dalchini*) sticks

4 cups / 1 lt / 32 fl oz Coconut milk (extracted from ¾ coconut)

300 gm / 11 oz Potatoes

Salt to taste

METHOD

- Blend the curry powder with 1 cup water.
- Heat the oil in a pan; fry the shallots, garlic and ginger pastes until fragrant. Add in the curry powder mixture and fry further.
- Add the beef with a little bit of water. Add cloves, pounded fried coconut, star anise, and cinnamon sticks. Stir slowly and add the coconut milk, potatoes, and salt. Simmer until the potatoes are cooked.
- Serve the beef curry hot with plain steamed or with bread or roti.

Madira

This dish was so famous that a poet wrote: "Madira is the festive tray, Is like the moon in full array, Madira cannot rivalled be, To heal the sick man's malady, Tis as delicious as Tis good, A very miracle of food."

INGREDIENTS

SERVES 4-6

1 kg / 2.2 lb Chicken boneless, cleaned, washed, cut into small pieces

1 Leek

2 Onions, medium-sized, peeled

½ tsp / 1½ gm Coriander (*dhaniya*) powder

½ tsp / 1½ gm Cumin (*jeera*) powder

½" Cinnamon (*dalchini*) stick

¼ tsp *Mastic* (see note)

1 cup / 250 gm / 8 oz Yoghurt (*dahi*), whisked

¼ tsp Lemon (*nimbu*) juice

½ cup / 30 gm / 1 oz Mint (*pudina*), fresh, chopped

Salt to taste

METHOD

- Cook the chicken with enough water to cover until tender.
- Add leek, onions, coriander powder, cumin powder, cinnamon stick, and *mastic*; cook on medium heat until rest of the water has been absorbed.
- In a bowl transfer the cooked chicken with vegetable and spices. Remove the cinnamon stick.
- Add yoghurt to the chicken mixture and blend well.
- Check seasoning and add little lemon juice and mint. Serve with bread.

Note: Mastic: *These gum drops are used in cooking and for baking. The hard resin can be ground and used to enhance the flavour of meat, sauces, cheese, and fish.*

Pandang Chicken

A classic dish of Indonesia. Indonesian dishes are among the most delicious in the world. This dish can be made earlier then required to allow the flavour to seep in, and heated just before serving.

INGREDIENTS

SERVES 4-6

1 kg / 2.2 lb Chicken, boneless, cut into 3" cubes

½ cup / 120 ml / 4 fl oz Lemon (*nimbu*) juice

250 gm / 9 oz Tomatoes, ripe, made into purée

3 Red chillies, small, seeded, sliced into thin strips

2 tsp / 12 gm Ginger (*adrak*), fresh, grated

2 Garlic (*lasan*) cloves, crushed

1 tsp / 3 gm Turmeric (*haldi*) powder

1 Lemon grass, 10 cm long

1 cup / 250 ml / 8 fl oz Coconut cream

METHOD

- Marinate the chicken with lemon juice for about 1 hour.
- Cook the tomato purée in a pot with red chillies, ginger, garlic, turmeric powder, lemon grass (remove stem before serving), and chicken along with the marinade. Bring to the boil, reduce heat, cover and simmer for 30 minutes.
- Add coconut cream and simmer, uncovered, for 10 minutes. Remove and serve hot with steamed rice.

Rubyan Mishwi

A great dish to put before your family. The tomato sauce provides a base for the prawns. It is neither too strong nor too spicy. Served with saffron rice, it gives an extra fragrance and a charming appearance to the dish.

INGREDIENTS

SERVES 4-6

900 gm / 2 lb
Prawns, peeled

5 Ripe tomatoes, medium-sized, peeled, chopped, puréed

½ tsp / 2½ gm
Cinnamon (*dalchini*) powder

Salt to taste

Black peppercorns (*sabut kali mirch*), freshly ground, to taste

3 Garlic (*lasan*) cloves, crushed

2 Onions, medium-sized, finely chopped

1½ tbsp / 25 ml
Refined oil

3 tbsp / 45 ml / 1½ fl oz
Lemon (*nimbu*) juice

Parsley, freshly chopped, for garnishing

METHOD

- Season the prawns with cinnamon powder, salt and black pepper.
- Sauté the garlic and onions in oil until soft. Blend in the tomato purée diluted with a little water, stirring well. Allow to simmer on gentle heat for about 12 minutes
- Add the prawns and cook on medium to high heat for about 10 minutes. Stir frequently and remove from heat when the prawns are tender.
- Sprinkle lemon juice, garnish with parsley and serve on a bed of saffron rice.

Black pepper

Most cuisines in the world are incomplete without this small black ball called black pepper also known as "home doctor". Its effect treats cold, cough, intestinal worms, and indigestion and brings relief from toothache. Its powder mixed with honey helps cure eczema.

Hanaakuri Hibaru

Maldive's delightful fish preparation which has exotic combinations of flavours ranging from sweet to hot and spicy to mild.

INGREDIENTS

SERVES 4-6

250 gm / 9 oz Swordfish, skinned, bones removed, cut into large cubes

¼ cup / 50 ml / 1¾ fl oz Coconut (*nariyal*) oil

50 gm / 1¾ oz Onions, finely sliced

10 gm Garlic (*lasan*) cloves, thinly sliced

1 piece *Rampe* leaf (see note)

2 Curry leaves (*kadhi patta*)

2 tbsp / 14 gm Curry powder

Salt to taste

METHOD

- Heat the oil in a pan; fry the onions, garlic, rampe leaf, and curry leaves until the onions turn golden brown. Add the fish together with the curry powder and salt to season.
- Braise the fish on low heat, covered, for 20 minutes. Toss the fish in the pot now and then. Do not stir, as this will break the tender flesh into pieces. Remove and serve hot.

Note: *Rampe leaf is also known as pandan leaf or screwpine leaf, mostly used in savoury and sweet dishes. It is commonly used in Sri Lanka, Malaysia, and Indonesia. Its essence is used to fragrant Indian curry dishes.*

Fish

Fish is good for those suffering with arthritis as it is rich in protein, potassium, vitamins, and minerals with only a moderate amount of sodium. It is believed that cod-liver oil is the best remedy to lubricate the joints. It also keeps the eyes bright and hair black.

Shorshe Ilish

Bangladeshis and Bengalis are known for their love of fish. Hilsa in mustard sauce is an exquisite dish whose taste cannot be forgotten for days together.

INGREDIENTS

SERVES 4

1 Hilsa (*ilish*) fish, cut into steaks

1 tbsp / 7 gm
Turmeric (*haldi*) powder

1 tbsp / 10 gm
Mustard seeds (*rai*) / Ground mustard paste

6 Green chillies

2 tbsp / 30 ml / 1 fl oz
Mustard oil

1 Onion, large, diced

1 tbsp / 7 gm
Red chilli powder

Salt to taste

METHOD

- Rub salt and turmeric powder on the fish steaks and set aside.
- If you use whole mustard seeds, ground them into a paste along with the green chillies and 1 tbsp water.
- Heat the oil in a flat-bottomed pan; sauté the onions until light brown. Add the mustard-chilli paste and red chilli powder and stir-fry for 2-3 minutes.
- Add ½ cup water, making sure you scrape any spices that are stuck to the bottom of the pan. Add the fish steak and cook covered on medium heat for about 10 minutes. Flip over the fish and cook covered for another 5 minutes until excess water has evaporated. Check for salt.

Mustard

Mustard is one of the oldest and most widely used spice. It has an important place in medicine. The Greek said it is a gift of god to mankind. Over the years it has been prescribed for scorpion stings, epilepsy and respiratory troubles. It helps sciatic or ache in the hip.

Dolma

Dolma is a Turkish word meaning to stuff or fill. This is a favourite Middle Eastern method of cooking vegetables such as eggplant, pepper, tomatoes, etc., whereby they are filled with lamb / chicken / rice / fruits and flavoured with a variety of nuts and spices.

INGREDIENTS

SERVES 4-6

25 Cabbage (*bandh gobi*) leaves

½ cup / 100 gm / 3½ oz Rice

a pinch Salt

1 tbsp / 15 ml Olive oil

1 Onion, medium-sized, finely chopped

1 Garlic (*lasan*) clove, crushed

1 tsp Mint (*pudina*), finely chopped

1 tbsp / 4 gm Parsley, finely chopped

a pinch Black pepper (*kali mirch*)

250 gm / 9 oz Lamb mince

1 cup / 250 ml / 8 fl oz Chicken stock

METHOD

- Blanch the cabbage leaves in boiling salted water for 3-4 minutes, drain and cut out thick centre of large leaves. Keep aside.
- Boil the rice in salted water until just tender, then rinse under cold running water and set aside to drain.
- Heat the oil and sauté the onion and garlic. Add mint and parsley; stir, add seasoning. Add the meat and fry until lightly browned. Remove from heat and leave to cool. Add the rice, and mix well.
- Spread one leaf on a board with wrong side up. Place about 1 tbsp of the meat mixture on each leaf then fold the two sides over the filling and wrap loosely. Repeat this process until all the leaves are stuffed. Arrange the stuffed rolls in a shallow pan.
- Add some oil and chicken stock. Cover and simmer for 45 minutes until tender. Serve hot.

Aur Jho Ras

This dish is nothing but a tangy curry, dominated by the flavours of garlic and mustard seeds and spiced up with just green chillies and tamarind. The best part of this dish is the gram flour rolls. Do not skip the rolls, as they actually add a wonderful dimension to the flavour of curry.

INGREDIENTS

SERVES 4

6-7 tsp Gram flour (*besan*)

1-2 tsp / 5-10 ml Refined oil

1 pod Garlic (*lasan*), peeled, crushed

2-3 Green chillies

2-3 tsp / 6-9 gm Mustard seeds (*rai*)

2 Radishes and potatoes (use only these), sliced or cubed

2-4 cups / 500 ml-1 lt Water

2-3 tsp / 10-15 gm Tamarind (*imli*) pulp

Salt to taste

¼ tsp Turmeric (*haldi*) powder

½ tsp / 1½ gm Red chilli powder

Green coriander (*hara dhaniya*) leaves for garnishing

METHOD

- Heat 1 tsp oil in pan; add garlic (save 2-3 cloves for later use) and green chillies. Stir-fry till the garlic turns soft but not brown.
- Add mustard seed and sauté for a few seconds. Add radish, potato chunks, and about 2 cups water. Add tamarind pulp, salt, and turmeric powder and boil for a few minutes. Reduce heat and simmer till potato is cooked
- Mix the gram flour with some salt, 2-3 crushed garlic (that was kept aside) and red chilli powder and knead to a stiff dough using little water.
- Make small oblong rolls of this dough (about 6-7) and drop them to the simmering *kadhi*.
- Cook for 15-30 minutes or until potato and gram flour rolls are cooked from the centre. Add water if required, this *kadhi* is of diluted consistency, and adjust the seasoning.
- Serve garnished with green coriander.

Kookoo-ye-Sabzi

This, the most famed *kookoo*, is prepared with fresh herbs and is traditionally served on New Year's Day in Iran.

INGREDIENTS

SERVES 4

2 Lettuce leaves, finely chopped

6 Spring onions (*hara pyaz*), finely chopped

2 Leeks, washed thoroughly, finely chopped

6 tbsp / 24 gm Parsley, finely chopped

3 tbsp / 12 gm Green coriander (*hara dhaniya*)

3 tbsp Spinach (*palak*), finely chopped,

3 tbsp / 45 gm / 1½ oz Butter

6 Eggs

½ tsp / 1½ gm Turmeric (*haldi*) powder

¼ tsp Cinnamon (*dalchini*)

½ Dilweed

Salt to taste

¼ tsp Black pepper (*kali mirch*)

3 tbsp / 30 gm / 1 oz Walnuts (*akhrot*), chopped

2 tbsp / 20 gm Raisins (*kishmish*)

METHOD

- Melt the butter in a large frying pan. Add the lettuce, spring onions, leeks, parsley, green coriander, and spinach; fry for 5 minutes, stirring regularly.
- Meanwhile, break the eggs into a bowl. Add the remaining ingredients and mix well. Pour the egg mixture into the pan and mix well.
- Bake in the centre of an oven preheated to 180° C / 350° F, gas mark 4 for about 45 minutes or until set and lightly golden.
- Remove cut into wedges and serve hot or cold.

Dal Akbari

An exotic recipe of simple lentil from the imperial kitchen of Emperor Akbar. This recipe is taken from *Ain-e-Akbari*–a gazetteer of the Mughal empire detailing every aspect of Akbar's government written by his courtier Abul Fazl.

INGREDIENTS

SERVES 4

3 cups / 600 gm / 22 oz Yellow lentil (*toor dal*), split, skinned

Salt to taste

¼ cup / 60 gm / 2 oz Yoghurt (*dahi*), hung

2 tsp / 10 ml Ginger (*adrak*) juice

4 Cloves (*laung*)

1 tsp Cardamom (*elaichi*) seeds

½" Cinnamon (*dalchini*) stick

4 tbsp / 60 gm / 2 oz Ghee

2 Onions, sliced

1 tbsp / 15 ml Lemon (*nimbu*) juice

¼ tsp Saffron (*kesar*), dissolved in milk

Gold leaf (*varq*) for garnishing

METHOD

- Boil the lentil with 1 tsp salt and drain.
- Add yoghurt and ginger juice and leave aside for 15 minutes.
- Grind cloves, cardamom, and cinnamon to fine powder. Sieve and keep aside.
- Heat the ghee in a pan; fry the onions to golden brown; remove one-third of the onion to be used later. Add powdered spices and stir-fry. Add lentil mixed with yoghurt, and cook on low heat adding 1 cup water.
- When lentil is soft and cooked, add lemon juice and reserved brown onions crushed with hands. Sprinkle saffron, cover and cook on *dum*.
- Serve decorated with gold leaf.

Beranj aur Naan

(Rice & Breads)

Rice and rice-based dishes are the basic diet of most Muslim countries. A dish of rice cooked plain and then spiced with meat, poultry, nuts, and flavoured with aromatic spices such as saffron and with ghee added is called *pulao*. It can be scribed to Persian and Arabic *pilav*, *pulao*, *palov*, *pilaf* yet it would appear to have found its way all over Muslim world. Each *pulao* lends a totally unique flavour. Cooking and serving method of each *pulao* changes from place to place. It is cooked on *dum*, it is boiled in stock, and layered in a *handi*.

The history of **bread** starts with Neolithic cooks and marches through time according to ingredient availability, advances in technology, economic conditions, socio-cultural influences, legal rights (Medieval guilds), and evolving taste. The staff of life, bread, has been a major ingredient in all Muslim countries. Like variation in grains it has different methods of preparing it which differs from country to country. It is cooked in a tandoor–large clay oven, in an iron tandoor, on *saj*–a large circular dome-shaped piece of cast iron, on a *tawa*–a flat iron griddle or fried in a *kadhai*–wok. Breads were made sweet by adding sugar, they were made rich by adding milk, ghee, nuts and raisins, they were made colourful by smearing saffron. Some were baked simple and some were filled with lentil, meat, vegetables and dry fruits.

Methi ki Khichdi

A light, nutritious, inexpensive dish–a complete meal in itself. It is cooked on *dum* to retain its flavour. A favourite of the rich and poor, young and old. It is the first food of infants and also an offering to God.

INGREDIENTS

SERVES 4-6

1 kg / 2.2 lb Rice

125 gm / 4 oz Fenugreek seeds (*methi dana*), soaked overnight in cold water

4 tbsp / 60 gm / 2 oz Ghee

4 Cloves (*laung*)

1 Brown cardamom (*badi elaichi*)

2 Cinnamon (*dalchini*), ½" sticks

¼ tsp Black cumin (*shah jeera*) seeds

1 tsp / 6 gm Ginger (*adrak*) paste

1 tsp / 6 gm Garlic (*lasan*) paste

1 Onion, large, sliced

Salt to taste

METHOD

- Boil the fenugreek seeds in water and drain. Keep aside.
- Heat 3 tbsp ghee in a pan; add cloves, cardamom, cinnamon sticks, and black cumin seeds; stir-fry till they crackle. Add ginger and garlic pastes with ¼ cup water; stir-fry.
- Add the fenugreek seeds and fry. Add rice, salt and add 8 cups water. When the rice is done remove from heat.
- Heat 1 tbsp ghee in a pan; fry the onion and add to the cooked rice. Cover and cook rice on *dum* for 5 minutes.

Fenugreek

Fenugreek, also known as Greek Hay, is an amazing herb that is readily available in our kitchen. Many of us swear by the tasty *methi parathas* and can vouch for its taste, but still are ignorant of its medicinal properties and health benefits. The truth is that this powerful herb can cure a number of ailments, apart from serving as a beauty product.

Roz bil-loz wa bil-tamar

A simple and nutritive Bedouin dish, colourful and energetic to survive the hard desert life.

INGREDIENTS

SERVES 4-6

1 cup / 200 gm / 7 oz Rice

¼ cup / 50 gm / 1¾ oz Butter

50 gm / 1¾ oz Almonds (*badam*), blanched, halved

8 Dates (*khajoor*), stoned (they should be fresh, but dried ones will do, if plump)

50 gm / 1¾ oz Sultanas (*munakka*)

1 tsp / 5 ml Rose water (*gulab jal*), optional

METHOD

- Cook the rice and keep aside.
- Melt the butter in a frying pan. Add almonds, stirring until they turn golden. Now add the dates and sultanas, and cook, stirring, for a few more minutes. Remove from heat and mix in the rose water, if using.
- Pile the rice on a dish and arrange the mixture on top of it.

Flower Extracts

The culinary use of flowers and their extract dates back thousand of years with this first record mentioned in 140 B C. Many cultures of the world incorporate flowers and their extract to enhance fragrance and flavour of the dishes. Rose remains the most popular flower in use.

Whirling Dervishes Pulao

One of the recipes from the kitchens of Mevlaña Rumi. Mevlana treated food as a symbol to express the philosophy of life to his disciples. A simple pulao with no frills truly brings out the simple living of a dervish.

INGREDIENTS

SERVES 4-6

½ cup / 100 gm / 3½ oz Chickpeas (*kabuli chana*), soaked overnight with 1¼ cups water

1¾ cups Chestnuts

3 Carrots (*gajar*), medium-sized, cut into 1cm cubes

1 Onion, medium-sized

2 tbsp / 20 gm Pine nuts (*chilgoza*)

¼ cup / 50 gm / 1¾ oz Butter

1¾ cups / 350 gm / 12 oz Rice

500 gm / 1.1 lb Lamb boneless, cut into 2-2½ cm cubes

3 cups / 750 ml / 24 fl oz Water

Salt to taste

½ tsp Currants (*munakka*)

½ tsp / 1½ gm Black pepper (*kali mirch*)

½ tsp / 1½ gm All spice (*kebab chini*)

METHOD

- Add 1¼ cups of water to the soaked chickpeas and cook for 40 minutes in a pressure saucepan. Remove from heat and keep aside. Place in a saucepan. Cover and braise for 1 hour or until tender. Drain.
- Boil the chestnuts for 3-4 minutes. Peel while still hot, cool. Cut into 3-4 pieces. Add chestnuts and carrots to chickpeas. Cover and simmer for 20 minutes or until carrots are tender.
- Sauté onion and pine nuts in butter for 7-8 minutes in a covered pan. Stir in rice and meat. Sauté for few minutes, stirring constantly. Add warm water, mix well sprinkle salt and currant. Cover and simmer for 15 minutes.
- Add chickpea mixture again, cover and simmer for 5 minutes or until rice is tender, drain. Sprinkle with spices and remove from heat. Let it stand covered for 20 minutes before serving.

Couscous

Couscous is a grain made of semolina.The national dish of Morocco, which is of Berber origin. It is a dish superb in its simplicity and is one of the glories of Moroccan cuisine.

INGREDIENTS

SERVES 6

3 cups Assorted vegetables (potatoes, eggplant, carrots, pumpkin, string beans, peas, zucchini, tomato, etc.), cleaned, cubed or sliced

1 cup Couscous

½ cup / 120 ml / 4 fl oz Olive oil

1 Onion, finely chopped

½" Cinnamon (*dalchini*), stick

2 cups / 500 ml / 16 fl oz Vegetable stock

1-5 tsp *Harissa* (ia traditional Tunisian hot chilli paste–use as per taste)

5 cups / 1 kg / 2.2 lb Chickpeas, soaked, boiled

2 tsp / 10 ml Olive oil / Melted butter

1 tbsp / 4 gm Parsley, chopped

1 tbsp / 4 gm Green coriander (*hara dhaniya*), chopped

Black pepper (*kali mirch*) to taste

METHOD

- Heat the oil and sauté the onion and cinnamon stick on low heat, stirring occasionally for about 5 minutes or until onion is soft.
- Add potatoes, eggplant, and carrots (if using) and cook covered, stirring occasionally, for 10 minutes.
- Bring stock or water to the boil.
- Add pumpkin and *harissa* to the cooking vegetables, then 1¼ cups of the boiling stock, then the string beans, peas, zucchini, and chickpeas. Simmer, covered, for 15 minutes.
- Meanwhile, put the couscous in the bowl and pour remaining ¾ cup boiling stock over it. Stir in 2 tsp olive oil or butter and let it stand for 10 minutes. Steam for 5 minutes.
- Add tomato, parsley, green coriander and pepper to the vegetable sauce and serve over the couscous.

Sheermal

A popular bread of the Indian sub-continent for banquets and parties. The name is derived from a Persian word meaning dough, kneaded with milk. *Sheer* literary means milk and *mal* is for kneading. The bread is slightly sweet and cooked in an iron tandoor.

INGREDIENTS

SERVES 4-6

4¼ cups / 500 gm / 1.1 lb Refined flour (*maida*)

2 cups / 500 ml / 6 fl oz Milk

a pinch Salt

30 gm / 1 oz Yeast, dissolved in ¼ cup lukewarm water

1¼ cups / 250 gm / 8 oz Ghee

Yoghurt (*dahi*), thinly whisked for brushing

Warm milk for sprinkling

METHOD

- Heat the milk to lukewarm, keep stirring.
- Sieve the flour and salt together in a large bowl. Add yeast and milk, knead to a smooth dough. Cover with a wet cloth and leave aside for 4 hours in a warm place to rise. Add ghee and punch down the dough with fists.
- Divide the dough into 6 equal portions and shape into round balls. Place each round in a floured board, roll into 4"-diameter round-thick circle. Place the circles on a greased iron tray and prick all over with a fork, leaving 1" margin around.
- Smear the surface with yoghurt and cook in moderate oven. Remove when half done and sprinkle cold milk well over both sides, as this makes the roti soft, put them back to the oven and cook again to golden colour.

Khajoor aur Anjeer ki Roti

Suitable for *suhoor*, the before sunrise meal of Ramadan.

INGREDIENTS

SERVES 6

1 cup / 150 gm / 5 oz Dates (*khajoor*), chopped, pitted

1 cup / 150 gm / 5 oz Figs (*anjeer*), dried, chopped

¼ cup / 50 gm / 1¾ oz Unsalted butter, softened

1½ tsp / 7 gm Baking soda

1 cup / 250 ml / 8 fl oz Boiling water

½ cup / 100 gm / 3½ oz Sugar

½ cup / 60 gm / 2 oz Walnuts (*akhrot*), chopped

2 Eggs

¾ cup / 90 gm / 3 oz Refined flour (*maida*)

1 cup / 150 gm / 5 oz Wholewheat flour (*atta*)

½ tsp / 3 gm Baking powder

½ tsp / 1½ gm Salt

METHOD

- Preheat oven to 175° C / 350° F. Lightly grease an 8 x 4" baking pan.
- In a medium bowl, combine the dates, figs, butter, and baking soda. Pour in the boiling water, stir well and let it stand for 15 minutes.
- Beat the sugar, walnuts, and eggs into the date mixture. Combine the refined flour, wholewheat flour, baking powder, and salt; stir into the date mixture till well blended. Pour batter into the prepared pan.
- Bake in preheated oven for 55-65 minutes or until a toothpick inserted in the centre of the loaf comes out clean. Cool in the pan for 10 minutes, then turn out onto a wire rack to cool completely.

Figs

Figs are a top source of fibre, as well as potassium and vitamin B6. Fibre results in bulkier stools, which lessen the incidence of constipation, hemorrhoids and colon cancer. Fibre also lowers cholesterol and the risk of heart disease.

Barbari

The most famous and widely used bread in Iran, *barbari* is a part of Iranian culture. A piece of *barbari* with some feta cheese and a cup of tea form the traditional breakfast in Iran.

INGREDIENTS

SERVES 4

3 cups / 360 gm / 12 oz Refined flour (*maida*)

1½ cups / 375 ml / 13 fl oz Water

2¼ tsp / 10 gm Active dry yeast

1 tsp / 6 gm Baking powder

1 tsp / 3 gm Salt

Cornmeal or wholewheat flour for dusting the baking sheet

Poppy seeds or Sesame seeds or Black sesame seeds (optional) for sprinkling on bread

For the romal sauce:

1 tsp Refined flour

1 tsp / 6 gm Baking soda

⅓ cups / 80 ml / 2½ fl oz Water

METHOD

- Dissolve the yeast in 100 ml warm water and let it stand for 3 minutes.
- Mix the flour, baking powder, and salt together.
- Pour the yeast mixture and the rest of the water into the centre of the flour and knead for 15 minutes to make a smooth dough.
- Divide dough into 2 round pieces. Slightly sprinkle the baking sheet with wholewheat flour and transfer the pieces to it. Cover and leave them in a warm place for 1½ hours or until doubled in bulk.
- Mix all ingredients of romal sauce and bring to the boil. Let it cool down before using it.
- Brush the dough with the sauce, using fingers punch dough in a straight line. Brush dough with the sauce one more time and sprinkle with poppy seeds. Let it stand for 45 minutes.
- Meanwhile preheat the oven to 180° C / 375° F. Pull the dough with your hand to make it longer. Bake for 30 minutes or till golden.

Flat Bread

Flat breads are known to have been baked in settlements from the Euphrates Valley in Iraq where a baker's oven from 4,000 B C was excavated on the site of Babylon, all the way down to Egypt where they are recorded on tomb inscriptions dating from 3,000 B C. The most basic are still a mixture of flour, water and salt kneaded into a pliable dough before being shaped by hand and baked. Wheat is the most popular choice of grain although barley, millet, corn, oats, rice and rye are also used to make various flat breads.

Halviyat aur Sharbat

(Desserts & Beverages)

There is a popular saying: "To be in Arab and not have a sweet tooth is to be a Muslim and not believe in paradise." Most of the desserts are milk based. The oldest known Islamic sweet meat is *faludhaj*, a Persian concoction of ground almonds, sugar, rose water, and milk, which is said to have been introduced in Mecca, to cater for pilgrims making the Haj. Later many rich sweet meats were added.

Pastries, desserts, *halvas* and *murabbas* are important sweets of the Muslim world and are made in abundance for any occasion. These desserts are exciting and original and a housewife takes pride in its making.

Sweets figure in many prominent dates in the Muslim calendar–first day of Muharram, the Prophet's birthday, Eid-ul-Fitr, and Shab-e-Barat. Interestingly each festival has a particular sweet dish and people wait the whole year to eat it.

Sharbats are important aspect of Muslim cuisine. The most common kind is combination of sugar and water. There are many kinds of sharbats: to quench thirst, to give energy or just to refresh on hot summer days. Vendors all over the Muslim world carry a selection of colourful drinks made of fruits, yoghurts, tamarind, etc., chanting and calling customers to come and enjoy their drinks. Though recent years, modern lifestyle has changed the life of these vendors as sharbats of all kind are sold commercially in super markets.

Seviyon ka Muzzafir

No celebration of Eid-ul-Fitr is complete without this exotic milk dessert. It is prepared at the crack of dawn before the morning prayers.

INGREDIENTS

SERVES 4

170 gm / 6 oz Vermicelli (*seviya*), fine

¾ cup / 150 gm / 5 oz Ghee

6 Green cardamom (*choti elaichi*), crushed

3 Cloves (*laung*)

1-2 cups / 250-500 ml / 8-16 fl oz Milk

2¾ cups / 350 gm / 12 oz Sugar

1 cup / 250 ml / 8 fl oz Water

100 gm / 3½ oz Wholemilk fudge (*khoya*)

¼ tsp Saffron (*kesar*), warmed, ground

4 drops Screwpine essence (*kewra*)

For the decoration:

12 Pistachios (*pistas*), cut into slivers

2 sheets Silver leaves (*varq*)

METHOD

- Heat the ghee on medium flame in a frying pan; add green cardamom and cloves. Stir-fry. Add vermicelli, lower heat, and fry to an even light brown colour. Remove vermicelli to a deep saucepan.
- Add milk, a little at a time, and cook on low heat till vermicelli is cooked. Remove from heat.
- In a separate saucepan, make sugar syrup of two-string consistency by boiling the sugar and water together. Add wholemilk fudge, saffron, and screwpine essence; mix well but gently. Simmer on low heat till the liquid has dried. Spoon on the vermicelli.
- Decorate with pistachios and silver leaves.

Rangeenaq

A rich but energetic dessert made of dates, colourful to look at and easy-to-make.

INGREDIENTS

SERVES 6

1 kg / 2.2 lb Dates (*khajoor*), seeds removed, chopped into small pieces

½ cup / 100 gm / 3½ oz Ghee

2 cups / 500 ml / 16 fl oz Milk

2 cups / 500 ml / 16 fl oz Water

4 Green cardamom (*choti elaichi*), powdered

12 Pistachios (*pista*), blanched, coarsely chopped

12 Almonds (*badam*), blanched, coarsely chopped

12 Cashew nuts (*kaju*), coarsely chopped

METHOD

- Heat the ghee in a wok (*kadhai*); fry the dates for a few minutes. Add the milk and simmer, on low heat, adding water as required to soften the dates.
- Mash the dates to pulp, and add green cardamom powder. Simmer for a minute. Add pistachios, cashew nuts, and almonds; mix well.
- Cook for 1-2 minutes to a porridge-like consistency. Cool and serve with cream.

Dates

An Arabian fruit, cultivated for over 4,000 years is a staple source of food for the Bebouins, and one of the main ingredient in true Arab cooking. It has tremendous healing properties especially for people suffering with heart problems. The nicotine content in dates helps to cure intestinal infection.

Sheer Berenj

This milky dessert has travelled miles and is popular throughout the Muslim world.

INGREDIENTS

SERVES 6

½ cup / 100 gm / 3½ oz Rice, short grain, rinse if necessary

1½ cups / 375 ml / 13 fl oz Cold water

4 cups / 1 lt / 32 fl oz Milk

¼ cup / 50 gm / 1¾ oz Sugar, granulated

a pinch Salt

2-3 tsp / 10-15 ml Rose water (*gulab jal*)

½ tsp / 1½ gm Green cardamom (*choti elaichi*), powdered

Honey for serving optional

METHOD

- Place the rice in a heavy pan with water and bring to the boil, stirring occasionally. Boil gently, uncovered, for 15 minutes or until the water is absorbed.
- Stir in milk, add salt and bring to a slow simmer. Simmer gently, uncovered, until pudding is thick. Take care that the pudding does not scorch. Stir occasionally with a wooden spoon.
- Add sugar, rose water to taste, and green cardamom powder. Stir to blend.
- Serve in individual bowls warm or chilled with a little honey drizzled on top, if desired.

Saffron

As an ingredient in both ancient and traditional medicines, saffron has long been used as a healing agent. Known for its effective antibacterial and antiviral properties, it is considered effective against stomach pains, coughs, and chronic bronchitis, and can also prevent tooth decay.

Sekanjabin

It is a concoction loved by people all over the Muslim world. A cool drink for a hot summer day to quench your thirst.

INGREDIENTS

SERVES 6

1 cup / 250 ml / 8 fl oz Lemon (*nimbu*) juice, fresh

1 cup / 200 gm / 7 oz Sugar

5 cups / 1¼ lt / 40 fl oz Water

½ tsp / 1½ gm Black salt (*kala namak*)

2 Rind of lemons

3 tbsp / 12 gm Mint (*pudina*), fresh, chopped

METHOD

- Dissolve the sugar in 1 cup water and cook on low heat, stirring constantly to make syrup. When the syrup is of one-string consistency remove from heat and keep aside to cool.
- Add lemon juice when liquid is of room temperature. Add 3 cups of water and mix.
- Add black salt and lemon rind while serving. Can be served with club soda.
- Garnish with mint leaves

Lemon

Lemon has remarkable healing properties. It is not only a natural appetizer and natural aid for digestion and weight loss, but is also a natural internal body cleanser. Lemon rightly deserves to be called a superfood as each lemon is packed with powerful antioxidant and anti-cancer healing properties.

Badam ka Sharbat

It is a popular drink served on the tenth day of Muharram. It can be preserved in the refrigerator for many weeks and can be served with milk or water.

INGREDIENTS

SERVES 6

½ cup / 60 gm / 2 oz
Almonds (*badam*), soaked overnight, peeled, ground to paste

1 cup / 200 gm / 7 oz
Sugar

1 cup / 250 ml / 8 fl oz
Water

12 Green cardamom (*choti elaichi*)

METHOD

- Add sugar and 1 cup water to the almond paste and cook. Bring to the boil slowly.
- Grind the green cardamom, unpeeled, and tie them in a muslin cloth and add to the almond syrup. Stir constantly. When syrup is a little thick, of two-string consistency, remove from heat and keep aside to cool. Remove cardamom tied in muslin cloth and discard. This is a concentrated almond syrup.
- While serving, add 2 tbsp almond syrup to one glass of milk. Sprinkle cardamom powder and a few rose petals and serve cold.

Almond

This drink increases energy in the body, quenches thirst and cures cough. Almond contains all the required vitamins, which are necessary for the growth of a body and mind but should not be used in excess, as it can cause indigestion.

Ayran

A popular drink all over Turkey. It is always served chilled as a refreshment during summer.

INGREDIENTS

SERVES 6

3 cups / 750 gm / 24 oz Yoghurt (*dahi*)

2 cups / 500 ml / 16 fl oz Milk

2½ cups / 625 ml / 20 fl oz Water

1½ tsp / 4½ gm Salt

METHOD

- Place the yoghurt in a bowl. Beat with a fork until well blended.
- Add milk, gradually, mixing well.
- Stir in ice-cold water and salt; mix well and serve.

Yoghurt

Yoghurt is rich in potassium, calcium, protein, and B vitamins, including B-12. Research shows yoghurt strengthens and stabilizes the immune system. The lactobacillus in yoghurt feeds the intestines, maximizes nutrients you can absorb into your body, and insures the digestive system stays healthy.

Tulsi ki Chai

This is a traditional tea that has been the Indian drink of choice for hundreds of years. *Tulsi ki chai* is a delicious, satisfying and healthy beverage.

INGREDIENTS

SERVES 6

3 tsp Green tea

a handful Fresh basil (*tulsi*) leaves

Sugar to taste

METHOD

- Warm the teapot with a little hot water and pour out.
- Add the tea leaves and basil; pour a little hot water into the pot, swirl around and pour 900 ml / ½ pint boiling water into the pot.
- Serve in cups with sugar as per individual choice.

Basil

In the past centuries, basil was accorded wide respect for its healing potential and was used to purify the mind, open the heart, and even cure malaria. Today, herbalists recommend basil as an antispasmodic. It is, therefore, often used to treat intestinal problems, motion sickness, flatulence and nausea. It also relaxes bronchial spasms and is thus helpful for treating various respiratory illnesses.

Index